How to Have Great Sex:

Both Sides of the Coin

By Wilson Sciubba
Copyright © 2013

© 2013 by Wilson Sciubba

ISBN-13:
978-1490468624

ISBN-10:
1490468625

First Printing, 2013

Printed in the United States of America

Income Disclaimer

This book contains business strategies, marketing methods and other business advice that, regardless of my own results and experience, may not produce the same results (or any results) for you. I make absolutely no guarantee, expressed or implied, that by following the advice below you will make any money or improve current profits, as there are several factors and variables that come into play regarding any given business.

Primarily, results will depend on the nature of the product or business model, the conditions of the marketplace, the experience of the individual, and situations and elements that are beyond your control.

As with any business endeavor, you assume all risk related to investment and money based on your own discretion and at your own potential expense.

Liability Disclaimer

By reading this book, you assume all risks associated with using the advice given below, with a full understanding that you, solely, are responsible for anything that may occur as a result of putting this information into action in any way, and regardless of your interpretation of the advice.

You further agree that our company cannot be held responsible in any way for the success or failure of your business as a result of the information presented in this book. It is your responsibility to conduct your own due diligence regarding the safe and successful operation of your business if you intend to apply any of our information in any way to your business operations.

Terms of Use

You are given a non-transferable, "personal use" license to this book. You cannot distribute it or share it with other individuals.

Also, there are no resale rights or private label rights granted when purchasing this book. In other words, it's for your own personal use only.

How to Have Great Sex:

Both Sides of the Coin

By Wilson Sciubba

Table of Contents

Introduction

Who doesn't want to learn how to have great sex?

Gone are the days where sex was viewed as something never to be discussed. Even in the bedroom sex was thought to be an act that was just "done." People didn't talk comfortably and openly about what they wanted and desired with sex. A "lady" would-n't tell her partner that she wanted him to slip his fingers into her and suck on her nipples. The unwritten rules of times past dictated women were reserved and quiet. They had a "duty" in the bedroom to service their man without any say whatsoever.

Times have changed and sex is even discussed in school. Chil-dren are learning earlier about all aspects of sex and experimenting openly in many cases. It isn't taboo to talk about sex openly, but rather encouraged.

Sex is a healthy part of life. Something that will better your mind, body and soul. Meaning it's a very good thing to have sex regularly regardless. This doesn't mean it's easy though. Great sex takes a whole lot of trial and error, learning, and communication to start. Feelings, wants, needs and desires need to be discussed openly, honestly and vividly. If you want to add to your knowledge of how to have great sex, this books for you.

The Science of Sex

If you are looking for the ultimate in mind/body experience, sex is it. Sure the focus in Sex-Ed class was the penis and vagina. But the reality is sex can and arguably should engage all parts of your body. This takes sex far beyond the scope of just the physical act. Now you may have been conditioned to associate sex with the heart or love. Which just isn't the case at all because sex is directed by the brain.

Scientific research tells us sexual attraction can give your body a mind of its own. Dilated pupils are one uncontrollable factor. Another is those icky sweaty palms. Where your norepinephrine in the brain works overtime and makes your sweat glands sprint.

It's also important to note the brain, sexual attraction and the dopamine reward system are all intricately connected. This is where your dopamine network attains satisfaction or pleasure of seeing the object of desire. It's true this "feeling" can turn addictive. Is that good or bad? Well that all depends.

Science also knows the nose knows. Your natural body scent is silently signally to the elite candidates whether they should move in for a closer look or head for the hills.

HEADS

Men are searching unconsciously for women that are ovulating and fertile. Procreating is what the body is intrinsically saying.

Scientific research tells us sperm are ejaculated from the penis at 28 miles an hour. With 120 million sperm making the grand exit or entrance, depending.

Kissing with sexual meaning dates back to 1000 B.C. This proof of affection also also allows men to pass on testosterone through saliva exchange. Letting both bodies know of the sexual intentions on the table, or bed.

TAILS

With regards to smell, women are looking for sweet smelling men because they are typically the strongest immune wise. Fittest of the fit wins naturally.

Science says there is an area called behind the left eye that works less when a woman climaxes or has an orgasm. This area is linked with what she thinks of herself. So orgasms will help to relax the natural criticism within and enable her to focus on the matter at hand, which is traditionally in the bed.

Scientific studies conclude that stimulating the clitoris instead of just penetrating is going to increase the chance of orgasm by up to 90%. This makes sense as there are over 8000 nerve endings in the clitoris.

EVOLUTION OF SEX

It's time for us to talk about the birds and the bees. Sex is something animals do, people do it and pretty much every organism on earth does. But don't think for one minute the only purpose of sex is pleasure. Evolution proves this just isn't the case at all. Let's look at organisms for instance.

Organisms

They often end up exerting gynormous amounts of energy just grabbing the attention of a particular hottie. Something they aren't doing just because they want some pleasure. This is a very stressful endeavor. In the cell, female and male genomes need to get it on without any mistakes. The gametes have to promote compatible unions while ensuring they don't stray toward other species. It's a communal effort because in each step internal conflict must be resolved in the best interests of the species as a whole. In other words it can't be about ME, ME, ME.

Asexual Reproduction

Here you've got a copy and divide methodology. Which looks to be effective, efficient and clean. Interestingly, biologists are perplexed with the fact sexual reproduction is definitely the dominant mode. Which means there must be some sort of evolutionary benefit or gain with it. Of course the water isn't clear here, just muddy.

The main questions arising from all this for scientists to "figure out," are:

13

* Why is sex so persuasive in the natural world and why did it evolve in the first place?
* How do these intricate sexual systems evolve?

Scientists believe it's all about naturally making a species strong. This is achieved through genetic recombination, where harmful mutation has the chance to be removed and stronger combinations created. This will improve the viability of a species. The stronger do survive perspective.

Scientists have also discovered that needs to be both a physical and internal attraction for a successful union to occur. All of which is influenced by various other factors including social conflict balancing.

Let's take this scientific information and move it back into caveman time.

THE CAVEMAN DAYS

It makes sense the purpose of sex, both scientific and logical, was to procreate. In order to survive the species at hand needed to engage in sex to reproduce and make more.

When it comes to humans, it really does seem pretty straight forward. Moving back in time a few hundred years people didn't have the modern conveniences we have today. If they were hungry they couldn't just call up the local pizza delivery boy and order a large deluxe with extra cheese and have it delivered to their door.

They had to work for their food and it definitely wasn't easy. In fact their work revolved around hunting and preparing food and shelter, oh, and of course sex.

It wasn't sex for fun. It was sex with a purpose. If these people didn't create more of their species they would eventually become extinct. For example, they didn't have the medicines we have today to get a handle on disease. One outbreak of malaria could wipe out a whole tribe seemingly instantaneously.

If these tribes wanted to increase their chance of surviving they had to make babies. And lots of them. This leads to the point of purpose.

HEADS

Way back in the day men were programed to survive. It didn't make sense from this point of view to mate with one woman and produce a child a year if you were lucky. When you had the option of mating with many women and having five, six or more children each year. So the argument here is evolution supports the fact men are being programmed from the beginning of time to want to spread their fertile seeds throughout the community. Not just with one woman.

This evolutionary fact also supports the fact that men view sex differently than most women, or at least they have the ability to. Emotion doesn't have to be attached to the act of sex. Men were programmed with this ability to separate the two so they could ensure naturally the strong survived. Some people believe this to be true and others think it's just an excuse for those perpetual cheaters of the world. Definitely something to ponder.

TAILS

The flip side of the coin is the woman's evolutionary reality. Scientists believe women were programmed with the emotional ability that is necessary to raise children strong. Women are born with the intrinsic need to have children. Just think about that biological clock aging women talk about. Particularly

15

those that haven't had any children yet. If it wasn't pro-grammed, why do women talk about it?

The thinking is, a woman looks out for the best interest of the "family." Naturally looking for a mate that is fertile, strong and able to provide. One that will stand the test of time and always make sure the basics were provided for growth. Evolution dictates one main difference arises with the emotion factor. Men are able to literally separate the emotion and the physical part of sex if they want. Women aren't so good at it and this causes conflict. Women are searching for a monogamous union whether they want to admit it or not. It's just how women were made. Men are different.

And who's going to argue with science?

*Afterthoughts - Evolution is there for a reason. Men and women are different for a reason. These differences are what brings both together, often finding unified reasons for sex, sometimes not. Sex is necessary, pleasurable and something that is ever diversified. Let's leave it at that for now.

Types of Sex

Sex is multifactorial for lack of a better word. Sex encompasses a multitude of different kinds of sexual acts. That said, "sex" officially means anything sexual that leads to any sort of pleasure.

Oral Sex

Defined, oral sex is stimulating a person's genitals with your mouth.

HEADS

You probably have heard the term "Blow Job" when describing oral sex for a man. This is actually the made up slang term for fellatio, which is oral sex performed on a male. Contrary to the terminology used, there's no "blowing" involved. It's normally sucking and licking. In fact, blowing would actually be dangerous.

The How

Some men like it fast and dirty and others slow and sensuous. There are no rules and communication is key.

* Start Clean - Society seems to think it's the woman's genitals that are strong in scent and taste. Truth is men can smell and taste the same or stronger. It's good to start clean and if you'd like you can always use a flavored lubricant or perhaps a specialty flavored condom if you'd like to be safe and less messy.

* Relax and get comfortable. You can take the pole position here or give it up. If you want to feel powerful you can have him lay on his back and you can lay or crouch between his legs. If he's sitting on the bed you can kneel on a pillow facing him between his legs. This one does give him the option of pushing his penis forward into your mouth. Just something to keep in mind. He can also be standing in this position. Again you need to have a trust level you're comfortable with.

The stairs also works well. Maybe lay towels down to help prevent minor injuries and to keep it clean. The key here is communication. Knowing each other's preferences and tolerances is important.

* Arouse him first with some teasing - It's time for you to take the reins here and explore a little. With your hands first tease him. Rub him gently along the inner thigh, testicles, penis and perineum area. Watch closely his physical and verbal expressions in accordance to where and how you touch him.

Normally the tip of the penis, or glans is most sensitive. Along with the indentation spot between the glans and the shaft on the underside of the penis. Don't be afraid to take your time here and make him want it more.

* Lick followthrough - Now it's time to do the same teasing touch with your tongue. Go slowly and seductively with lots of saliva. If you aren't okay with the taste you can use flavored condoms or lube.

* Slowly take him in your mouth - Guide your lips over his penis when he's partially erect. Be careful to cover your teeth with your lips. Take him in your mouth as far as you're comfortable and be sure to keep your lips and mouth firmly to his penis. This gives him more sensation as you glide up and down his penis.

The technique of taking his penis in your mouth partially erect helps when getting comfortable with the penis size, particularly if he's larger.

* Careful with depth - If you have a sensitive gag reflex you may have trouble taking the entire penis in your mouth, especially if his penis is larger. If this is a problem you can take the penis in your mouth as far as comfortable and use your hand for the rest.

* Combo technique - Mouth, tongue and hand techniques work well in covering all bases. Switch things up and read his body reactions. This will guide you as to when, where and how much. Licking up and down the penis shaft is quite pleasurable. Then try sucking gently on the end of the penis while firmly but gently wrapping your hand around his penis while moving it up and down. This combined with the gentle sucking will drive him crazy. And don't be afraid to caress his testicles too. Or rub that sweet spot just on the underside of the testicles. It's extremely sensitive and can put him over the edge.

* Back off when he's coming - When a man starts to orgasm he usually doesn't need anymore help. Let him orgasm and re-charge for seconds.

* Swallow or not - This is just a personal preference. Not right or wrong. If you prefer not to, just make sure he knows it's nothing personal. When he's about to cum, remove your mouth and continue with your hand for a minute.

TAILS

Oral sex on a woman is technically "cunnilingus." The slang terms you may have heard are "eating out" or " going down." Some women enjoy oral sex more than vaginal, others do not. Again it's a personal preference. No right or wrong and com-munication with your partner is key.

The How

Oral sex on a woman can be incredibly intimate. There has to be a huge amount of trust and a comfort level that allows com-plete relation and focus. The mind needs to be in the right state if a woman is going to cum during cunnilingus. If you are go-ing to be skilled in giving oral sex to a woman you need to be good at reading bodily movements. Pay attention to how she responds and act accordingly. Be confident enough to ask and accept guidance to fine tune your skills. There's no "right" or "wrong" here, just continuous learning. What you are doing here is giving everything to your partner during oral sex. It's not about you, but rather all about her.

Note - 30 to 60 minutes is the recommended time. But full sat-isfaction can be achieved a whole lot quicker or longer than that if you wish. Communicate with her and figure out what works best.

* Hygiene first please - At the least, your hands and nails need to be clean. You don't want to be causing any infections because you didn't bother washing up. For all you gents that sport facial hair. If you've got facial hair that's okay. Just be sure you aren't in sandpaper mode. You don't need to be told that's going to hurt.

* Watered down helps - There are many people that are expecting a woman's vaginal area to be very strong smelling. If so, no worries. You can both slip in the bath or enjoy a shower together beforehand. Both of which will get your juices flowing and excite. Give yourself some time to get used to the taste. If it's not working for you flavored lubricants will. Just make sure you are both on the same page and no feelings are hurt.

* Slow and steady wins the race - Fast doesn't work so well here. It's important to pay attention, start slowly and ease your way into oral sex. With a little time you will get to know each other better and understand when she wants you to get nasty NOW. Other times it may take a while to "warm her up."

To start you should focus on things you know drives her crazy. You can't go wrong with kissing her neck and telling her how much you want and desire her. Explore her body with your hands and mouth - teasing and exciting her for what's to come. You'll know when it's time to dive in. Her hips will move with you and she will be moaning, handing control over to you. That's when the real fun begins.

* Get relaxed - If you're both comfortable the pleasure is only going to be better. Don't be afraid to try different positions. Pillows are excellent for getting those hard to reach angles that will set her on fire. You might try her laying on her back and you positioned comfortably between her legs. This gives her some control on positioning and angle, great for learning.

Another is having her lay on her stomach with a pillow under her hips for better access. You can position yourself comfortably between her legs. It's all about communication here and figuring out what works best for both of you. Diversity is key and trying different positions will keep the fires burning.

One other common position is her sitting back in an easy chair with her knees up by her head and legs spread. Of course you can be kneeling in front of her. This one enables her to watch you performing oral sex. For some that's just heaven.

* Know her body - If you skipped that Sex-Ed class you may want to brush up on the female genitalia. Most of your focus needs to be on the clitoris, the most sensitive part. Although this is where you are going to need to be open and communicative. Each woman is different and you are going to have to figure out what's sensitive and what isn't. Take a minute to spread her lips with your fingers and actually look at her labia, mons, vagina, anus and perineum, and clitoris.

* This is not a race - Many women have extremely sensitive clits, particularly if you are giving her oral sex just after having an orgasm with vaginal sex. So proceed with caution and take it slow. Do not dive right in and attack her clitoris.

Start by slowing licking her lips. Make sure you do this on the inside and the outside. Then move to the clitoris and vagina and don't forget to lick upwards from the perineum to the vagina. Pay attention to her body language. Is she moving her hips with you? Is she moaning? If you are unsure don't be afraid to ask her or have a secret signal, like a tap on the head. If you're really good she will be grabbing your head and pushing it down for more.

* Stick to the outskirts - Normally you don't have to uncover her clitoris to drive her into ecstasy. Many women love it when

you lick and suck their clitoris through the folds of the skin. It's extremely sensitive and her reactions will guide you.

* Don't be afraid to experiment - It's safe to say most women like a firmer touch with consistent strokes, but not always. Figure out what she prefers by testing the waters. Fast light tongue flicking can drive her crazy. But so can gentle sucking and rather firm and routine licking. Use your tongue in all directions. Circular motions, up and down, flickering, and so forth.

If she tightens up on you her body is just telling you to try something else. It's not personal so don't take it that way. Just shift your direction. You aren't going to improve your skills here unless you're willing to test the waters.

* Get her help - You can do one of two things here. If you've watched her masturbate before you will at least have an idea of how she likes to be stimulated. So use this information when you're giving her oral sex. Or you can ask her to take your hand and show you. Let her teach you how to stroke her. Faster, slower, firm or gentle.

* Multi-task with this - Your hands and mouth can both be exploring, stroking and pleasuring. Use your mouth to suck gently on her clit, nipple, or labia.

* Penetration will elevate excitement - Don't do this until she is excited. You can use a sex toy if you like or just your fingers. Lube them up and gently insert them into her vagina. Push them in and out rhythmically, varying the depth. Some women like it hard and deep, other faster and lighter. Make sure you are still using your mouth sucking or licking her clit.

Keep in mind the penetration factor sends some women straight over the edge. But it may not do much for others. Communicate with your partner and figure out what makes her lose control.

23

* Keep the rhythm - Women like rhythm with oral sex. It's important to not stop unless maybe you've got a kink in your neck or you need to catch your breath. When she's turned on you don't want to rock the boat. The "mood" can disappear fast.

You should be able to tell when she's ready to cum. Her moaning might increase, hips will rise up towards you, and she will start to clench her fists, arch her back, and tighten her body. Grabbing your head is another indication that she is about to climax. Don't worry, she'll let you know when she's finished.

Take note the clitoris is often EXTREMELY sensitive after an orgasm. Don't be surprised if she literally shoves your head away right after, your big head.

Toy note - It may take her a few minutes to climate or an hour or more. If you happen to get tired just take a break and replace your mouth with a vibrator or dildo to keep her stimulated while you regenerate.

A vibrator or dildo will also work great in combination with your fingers and mouth. Don't be afraid to experiment and figure out new ways to make her climax.

Vaginal Sex

This is what most people think of when they ponder "sex." Simply put it's when the erect penis of a man enters the vagina of a woman. With vaginal sex you can spread STDs and it's the only form of sex that may lead to pregnancy.

Guys seem to be the ones leading the way with vaginal sex. When they get excited or sexually aroused, their penis becomes erect and this signals they are ready for action. In order to relieve this "situation," a form of release works best. Natural instincts turn towards sex to increase their arousal level and enable them to ejaculate and physically relieve this "situation." Vaginal sex is one route to do this.

With an erection the penis swells and becomes erect because blood fills the corpus cavernosum. The main male indicator of sexual arousal.

TAILS

Vaginal sex is just as it sounds for a woman. It's where the penis penetrates the vagina. The purpose is for pleasure and of course baby making. When a woman is sexually aroused she naturally gets wet. There is increased blood flow to her vulva and clitoris. Along with "vaginal transudation" - which is the moisture that naturally seeps through the walls of the vagina in order to provide lubrication. A physical reaction that helps the body receive the penis smoothly and without friction. This natural lubrication is to ensure penetration isn't painful. As women get older and into menopause one physical change that seems consistent is dryness of the vagina. Lubrication is often used to help keep vaginal sex pleasurable.

* Incorporating sex toys into the act of vaginal sex is only going to add excitement and pleasure. Maybe she likes the sensations of a vibrator on her clitoris while you are penetrating her from behind? Or perhaps she has sensitive nipples and enjoys a combination of you sucking on them and vibrations while you are entering her. Communicate and explore because the only rules for her are the ones you make.

Anal Sex

Anal sex is something most people love or hate. Usually dependent on previous experience and comfort level. Some feel it's just plain dirty. Others have not had anal sex correctly and this can be very painful. When performed correctly anal sex

25

can be very pleasurable for both parties. As there are lots of sensitive nerve endings in the anal area.

That said, anal sex is also very risky. A woman can't get pregnant from anal sex but STD's can be transmitted. Particularly because of the increased likelihood of a tear and condoms breaking or coming off. If you are both disease free though it's perfectly safe.

The How

There are a few precautions which should be practiced with anal sex.

* Cleanliness is a priority - The anus has the function of keeping fecal waste in your body until it's ready to be released. It's full of germs so the area must be washed very well.

* It's pretty hard to get rid of all the germs in the anal area - It's wise to wear a condom during anal sex.

* Use lots of lube - The anus was made for waste to come out of, not in. So it's critical you use lots of lubrication to help avoid any painful tearing.

* Relaxed is critical - In order for anal sex to be void of pain she has to be completely relaxed. It's going to hurt otherwise. The best way to do this is to get her sexually excited. Oral sex works great to get her wet and ready. Before she climaxes try switching the focus to anal sex. Continuing to stimulate her clitoris with your fingers or a vibrator often works well.

HEADS

Again it's simply personal preference as to whether guys prefer anal sex over vaginal. For many guys it's just the "taboo" attached to anal sex that turns them on. The idea of dominance, prostitutes, control, pain, submissiveness, all thoughts that can awaken the loins, so to speak. Others may have trouble with anal sex for fear they may hurt their partner. Which is a valid concern.

There's always the size of the penis that may come into play. If the guy is rather large it may be physically hard to fit comfortably, even relaxed and with lots of lube. Another roadblock may be the length of the penis. Here you are just going to have to go very slow and test the waters.

The bottom line is, so long as you both "want" to experiment with anal entry sex, you can usually make it pleasurable, for him and her. Just be sure to communicate clearly and openly. Don't force anything and never take anything too personally. The emotions may get in the way of enjoyment here and that's okay. It's not the end of the world if anal sex isn't in the cards for you. Sex is about so much more than just that.

TAILS

For women there are some that see nothing exciting about having anal sex. There are women that choose never to try it because they think it's "dirty" or "lowly." Others have a more open perspective and if the cards align they won't hesitate to try it. Many of which end up getting pleasure from anal sex, even though it usually takes some getting used to.

Again the key is to make sure you, the woman, is "completely" relaxed. If you aren't it is going to hurt.

What some women do to get warmed up is to use a vibrator on their clitoris. They can even do this while their partner is performing anal sex. Exciting yourself sexually is going to relax you and this is one route to achieve orgasm while having anal sex, particularly if you're unable to cum with just anal sex.

It's important you guide your partner along here and take the time to get your juices flowing prior to anal penetration. Make sure your partner uses lubrication and communicate and guide him so it will be pleasurable for both of you.

Don't be surprised if this isn't your cup of tea right off the hop. All good things come to those that practice. Give it at least a few tries before throwing in the towel because anal sex truly can be a wonderful experience. But it's certainly not for everybody.

Phone Sex

Phone sex is pretty self explanatory. It's essentially a secret or "adult" conversation between two or more people. The act of sex is being described verbally by one or more people in the conversation. This sort of "sex" is a little harder, sorry, than let's say vaginal sex, because you need to tap into your imagination. The other person isn't there actually performing the sex acts with you. So you have to visualize sex using the descriptive words. Where you build up the sexual excitement through sexy talk, suggestive thoughts, and visually "thinking" about the other person performing the sex acts, on themselves or you.

At least one person masturbates at some point. A few of the different forms of phone sex are discussions on sex, guided, sexual sounds, suggestive talk, narration or performing the actual act while you are listening.

Phone sex can be used in various situations. Some couples use it regularly to add diversity to their relationship. Long distance relationships find this a fulfilling method of connecting between visits. There are also paying clients that use phone sex to fulfill their sexual urges. There's no right or wrong here. Whatever works for you is "right."

The How

Depending on your situation, there are different methods of executing phone sex. For simplicity we are going to use an anonymous phone sex conversation to learn how. So understand the caller is a beginner. Not really sure what to expect, feeling a touch awkward, and is looking to find a comfort level so they can release their sexual feelings.

* Use a headset - You may not think of this up front but having a headset means you aren't fumbling with the phone. You've got both hands free so you can avoid neck cramps and make the most of the conversation.

* Turn on the answering machine - The last thing you want to do is to be just about to explode and hear a "dingle-dingle" from your phone and recognize the ring as your mother. Talk about ruining the moment! Set your phone up to go automatically to your voice mail and turn off all other buzzers, ding-dongs and tones. No interruptions allowed during phone sex.

* Have a good start line - First impressions are important here. So when you initiate the conversation make sure you've got one rehearsed and ready, so nerves don't leave you tongue tied. "I wish you were here," is a good start line. If you can think of something better go for it.

* Be yourself - I know this one might be tough when you are uncomfortable. But it's important to try and not act like how you "think" you should act. In other words don't try talking manly sexy and extroverted when you are really a shy, timid gent. The operator is skilled in what "they" do. These people are professionals and will work with what you give them. They are skilled in this and this is what you are paying them for. So just be as "normal" as you can.

* Keep it filled - One sure thing during phone sex is that dead silence is just like sitting in a tub filled with ice. It will kill the moment in a flash. Now there may be instances without conversation, but they can be filled with a moan, sigh or other eroterotic noise to keep things moving along. Just make sure there is some sort of background noise consistently. And not the sound of your fingers gliding across the keys! It really is hard to start things from scratch.

* Moving to full sentences - The can be an intimidating move. By reading something sexy to your "partner," you can tell them what you'd like them to do to you. Or what you'd like to do to them without actually admitting this. That will come later.

* Start with the basics - You can start with basic genitalia descriptions. Use the words you learned in Sex-Ed class. Penis, clit, nipples, anus, vagina, are all great to start with. Simpler is better here, at least until you get used to everything.

* Get your "partner" involved - To get your "partner" involved in the action just ask them what they are doing. Perhaps you might ask them what they would do to you if they were there with you. It shouldn't take you long to get a "feel" for the comfort level of the operator and go with it. Obviously they are experienced, but this doesn't mean they aren't shy or a touch introverted. Different strokes for different folks.

* No laughing allowed - This one is a given but don't ever laugh or snicker at your partner because the mood is as good as gone if you do. This could very well make them self-conscious and that's just not a good thing if you're both looking to get off.

* Direction is important - Depending on who's leading the way the other person needs direction. So if the operator is talking you through getting you off and what she's saying is going to take you over the edge. Make sure you communicate this. "More," or "keep going," something to that effect should be

enough to hit the jackpot. If you don't let them know you are getting totally turned on, they may just stop and you'll be back to square one.

* Be confident - It doesn't matter what you are saying or doing for that matter during phone sex. Confidence is something that just has to be. If you're talking dirty, don't censor it, just talk dirty.

Follow these few basic guidelines and you should get exactly what you're looking for and more.

HEADS

Phone sex is nothing to be ashamed about. It works for some guys and not for others - so what? It's a personal preference and you never know unless you try, right? You'd be surprised the people that engage in phone sex with their partner or otherwise. Experiment, have fun, and test the waters to see if this is something that makes you a better you.

To get yourself in the "mood" you may want to read something erotically sexy or watch a porn. You know you and if this does it for you then go for it. Don't be afraid to leave all inhibitions at the door and let your "in the moment" out. If you feel like talking nasty dirty then do it. If you are stuck in an erotic fantasy don't be afraid to describe it. There is no right or wrong here and no judgment. Those are a few of the fabulous things about phone sex.

TAILS

Whether you are the giver, receiver, or both with phone sex, it's important to leave your manners at the door. This is all about role-playing, having fun and doing whatever it takes to get sexual pleasure without actually being with another person.

31

You need to relax, get comfortable, and tap into your wildest erotic imaginative thoughts.

The unknown is exciting and for women phone sex is all good. It can help to release stress and built up tensions, allowing you to enjoy the moment, or two, or three.

It's also important to sex aside any expectation you have of yourself. Allow your "turned on" mind and body to guide you and go with it. Don't try and slow or stop it because you think you should. If you're going to have great phone sex you've just got to go all the way.

*Afterthoughts - There are all sorts of different ways to have sex. Learning what you like, what your partner likes and how you both like it is important in figuring out how to have great sex. Whether you prefer oral, anal or vaginal sex really isn't the issue. Knowing "how" to find pleasure in the sex of choice and "how" to pleasure your partner is what's going to make it great.

What Sex Means

Sex can have very different meaning to guys and gals. It can also have different meanings within the word. Some differentiate "making love" and "having sex." Making love is usually about taking your time, lots of foreplay, kissing, hugging, cuddling, and attention to detail and each other.

Whereas "having sex" might be where you try and remove emotion and concentrate on physical satisfaction. Maybe these are the words you use to describe sex in a one night stand. Or perhaps when you have a "quickie," this is your definition. It really doesn't matter because in a healthy relationship you are lucky to have both. And that's just the beginning to having great sex.

HEADS

Maybe we have to go back to evolution here. But the fact is, men are programmed or wired differently than women. They are tuned naturally into procreating and seem to have an easier time removing emotion from the equation if need be. Many are seen as "stud muffins" if they are screwing 4 or 5 girls at a time. There's a status symbol of pride associated with men that have sex with lots of women. There's no right or wrong here, just different.

This doesn't mean men don't enjoy making love because most do. But they also seem to be eager to experiment with the flip side of the coin and have the "physical act" of the sex center stage more so than a woman. This just suggests that men may be naturally a little more open to phone sex than women, just because.

TAILS

Women are ingrained with the instinct of caring and nurturing. Built to have children and make sure they are taken care of. So this set thinking doesn't work as easily with phone sex. Not to say it's not something women do or enjoy, but it may take a little more mind convincing to make it happen.

Of course there's always going to be that pre-conceived notion that phone sex is only for the trouble makers, deviants of society. But this couldn't be further from the truth. Phone sex can be something just about any woman can enjoy giving or receiving and there's nothing wrong with either. It works for you or it doesn't, onward.

Don't be afraid to leave your worries at the door and test it out. Try it with your trusting partner or anonymously if you're too shy or don't happen to have someone right now. The purpose of phone sex is to enjoy the moment and release sexual tension. Nothing more less.

*Afterthoughts - Sex always has meaning. Whether it's a communication of love, revenge or just to make a baby. Take if for what it's worth because understanding and accepting the meaning behind sex is going to help you with achieving great sex every time.

Common Sex Issues and Solutions

It really is quite normal for both men and women to suffer from health issues that interfere with sexual pleasure, both giving and receiving. What you need to know is there is no reason to be embarrassed or ashamed about anything. Where there's a will there's a way. Rest assured there is a solution to just about every condition or mindset that interferes with your sexual performance and enjoyment of sex. You deserve to view sex as a fulfilling positive in your life. Here are a few common conditions that come with solutions. With a little time, patience, and treatment, you will be back in the saddle in no time.

HEAD
      * Erectile Dysfunction - More common than you might think, erectile dysfunction is the issue of not being able to keep

an erection long enough to have coitus, or being unable to get hard enough to perform sex.

Solution - First off, if you don't admit you have a problem with your penis and tell your doctor about it, then you're stuck with it. Often a better lifestyle in general will get rid of erectile dysfunction or in the least make it better. You can also try:

* Erectile Dysfunction Vacuums - This "penis pump" is used by many men and works quite well.

* Implants - Penile implants are a permanent solution for erectile dysfunction.

* There's also hormone therapy, supplements, herbs, and medication options

The bottom line here is to get help. Check with your doctor and figure out what works best for you and "do it!"

* Testosterone Deficiency - Another name for this is hypogonadism. It's where the body doesn't produce enough testosterone for normal sexual function.

Solution - Supplements are just one solution to this sex issue.

* Peyronie's Disease - This is simply and inflammation of the penis. It occurs in up to 10% of men.

Solution - Treatment options are medication and supplements, surgery, physical therapy and other devices. Speak with your doctor to find what works for you.

* Priapism - An often painful medical condition where an erect penis is always standing at attention. Even when there is no sexual stimulation in sight.

Solution - If your penis is staying erect for more than 4 hours and it's unwanted, you need medical attention. Sometimes medications are used or even a blood transfusion in specific cases. Your doctor will guide you here.

   * Ejaculatory Dysfunction - There are 4 kinds of issues here; premature ejaculation, delayed ejaculation, anorgasmia, and retrograde ejaculation. The problem is orgasming too soon, too late, not at all, or instead of ejaculating out the penis the ejaculation goes into the bladder.

Solution - Medications are often used in the treatment. Although sometimes it's a physical issue that needs addressing and this may require surgery and/or further investigation. Of course there's also the power of the mind that comes into play. Mental issues often trigger this sort of sex dysfunction and with proper counseling can be alleviated.

TAILS

It's not just men that have issues with sexual function and performance. Women have their fair share too. Some of which are:

* Emotional (stress, depression, body image, sexual trauma, relationship trouble) - The mind is extremely powerful and often directly affects sexual function, performance and perspective. And you only know what you know. So if a woman has had negative sexual experiences in her life this is going to influence the desire she has for sex in general and her ability to enjoy and explore sex and all it has to offer.

Solution - Counseling will help you get past any issues you may have faced with regards to sex. If you were sexually abused in any shape or form, this isn't something you can block out and get past on your own. It's important you find the courage to talk to a professional about it because otherwise it's going to interfere with your ability to enjoy and bask in the positive of sex.

       * Physical (injury, hormones, diabetes, arthritis) - Some of these are controllable and others aren't. If your hormones are out of whack you may not have a sex drive at all. You may have a physical injury that interferes with enjoyable sex. As you would after having an unfortunate car accident and are left recovering from a collapsed lung. Here you would have the inability physically to have enjoyable sex because your breathing is not 100%.

Conditions such as diabetes and arthritis are also situations that can interfere with sex in general.

Solution - It's so very important you confide with your doctor about all of your concerns here. You will need time to recover from any physical ailment that is interfering with sex. That's something which is just going to take time and patience. If you have a medical condition you can work with your doctor to figure out a solution. There is always a solution if that's what you want.

       * Natural Aging (dryness in the vagina, stiff) - Aging isn't fun for anyone. As a woman gets older and her cycle changes, her hormones go whacky and one result is a natural dryness in the vagina. This can turn pleasurable sex into painful sex if it's just left.

Solution - Hormone replacement is often used to help women deal with vaginal dryness and to minimize the "not fun" symptoms of menopause. That's a more permanent solution. You can always use lubrication get help things move along.

       * Medication - There are many medications that can interfere with a happy, healthy sex life. Medications can interfere with the natural function of the body. Blocking sex

hormones and increasing mood swings and fatigue, all of which can directly interfere with sex.

Solution - Working with your doctor you will be able to figure out a solution that works best for you. Sometimes it's as simple as adjusting your medication dosage or changing medications. Other times you may need to continue with your medication but adjust the times you are taking it, in accordance to when you have sex.

*Afterthoughts - Don't put off seeing your health care provider if you think you've got a physical ailment or condition that's interfering with sex. Take action and get control of it so you can move onto the focus of great sex.

Preferences

We are each individuals with unique genetic makeups and life experiences, sexual or otherwise. What's important is that you recognize and let your personal sexual preferences be known to your partner. This is important if you want them to please you during sex. It's all about communication and if you aren't willing to open your door here, then you likely aren't going to get the satisfying sexual experience you envision and truly desire.

HEADS

Based on that evolutionary stuff, here are some sexual preferences of men.

* The hunt for sex - Truth is, men are naturally on the hunt for sex. Otherwise they would just shut it down when it comes to women. In the absolute sense, men are hunters and an intrinsic quest set in them is to have sex. What's also important to note is that if a woman "gives it up" too quickly, many men will deem her not suitable for a long-term relationship, conscious or not.

* Men also don't want you to ever totally ignore their advances. Men are terrified of rejection in general and if you play hard to get too much, he's just not going to bother with you. Men don't want you to necessarily jump into their arms but you at least have to show them you have a little bit of interest in them sexually, if indeed that's the case.

* All men prefer variety - This one is true to a point. The proof is in the fact that most men have had a time where they've been with more than one woman. This doesn't mean that all men are going to screw around and want more than one woman though, just something for you to be aware of.

* Men want a woman that is strong but not unapproachable - If a woman is too proper or too strict this will deter a man from letting his mind wander. He will simply move on.

* A little bit of jealousy never hurts here - Men are fired up when they see other men interested in a particular woman. In other words, this is beneficial for a woman. In a marriage this can be used as an aphrodisiac and actually strengthen a union. For lack of a better word it can keep things spicy. Be careful though because if you cross the line here, it could backfire.

* Guys want to know how the girl feels - This one may come as a surprise but when it comes to sex men really do want to know what's in their partner's head. Men like to feel useful, wanted and desired. If they know and feel like they are pleasing their partner then they feel valued.

* Men want more open communication - Maybe it appears men are a little more bold in general when it comes to sex. Perhaps this is fact because they are more driven in general by their smaller head? The point here is men know the more open and honest and forthcoming a woman is, the better the sex will be. They don't like wondering and guessing, particularly when it

44

comes to sexual relations. Short, sweet and straight to the point is exactly what many men prefer.

* Cuddling is a good thing - Gone are the days when men "thought" they needed to show their manliness here and draw the line at admitting they liked to cuddle close after sex. It's not a sign of weakness. You see all humans need close physical contact intimately in order to be content. That's just a fact. As a baby we are cuddled close and this is an instinctive and intrinsic need for all human beings. It comes from within and never goes away. It feels good, gives us comfort and value, and helps us to gain strength. Guys may not always admit it but they really do like the cuddling after sex.

* Men prefer a girl that knows how to turn herself on - Often it takes a woman a little longer to get her sex juices flowing than a man. So they don't mind if you give yourself a bit of a head start so you're in the "mood" sooner rather than later. Not to mention if he gets to watch then you are only heating up the whole bed, not just your side.

* Keep it fun - Here's where you need to let loose a little and fly by the seat of your pants. Men prefer a woman that is able to just go with the flow. If anal sex just isn't working this time around you should be able to flip the switch and try something else without getting all caught up in it. This is a part of keeping sex fun and not getting too serious about it. Guys love this in a girl.

* "Good girls" be gone - I don't care how much of a princess you are. Guys want a girl that knows how to get nasty in bed. They prefer a woman that can step outside of herself and let loose her animal instinct. Not worrying about judgement. Men prefer at least a little bit of naughty when it comes to sex in general because this is only going to heighten their satisfaction and hers.

45

If it means talking dirty and playing the evil twin, then do it. You never know unless you try right?

* Diversity takes the cake - Men love to be challenged. When it comes to sex the unknown is alluring and sexy. So make certain you throw a curveball or two their way from time to time. Maybe he's just about to cum with you on top and you pull yourself off him and start giving him oral sex. It's just a thought. The idea is to always keep him guessing with the main goal of rocking his world - literally.

* Screw him when he least expects it - Maybe you show up at work and give him a blow-job in his office during his lunch? Or perhaps you take him into the family washroom at the mall and have coitus with him standing up. The idea here is men will go batty with a woman that isn't afraid to "sex-him" by surprise. The only limitations here are your imagination.

* Let him get straight to the point - A man likes a woman that will tell him to "take her" now. This is a complete turn-on and then some. You are communicating with your man that you are craving him and all hot and wet for him to explode deep inside of you. It's all about releasing the animal instinct in both of your from time to time. There's only good in that.

* Take control sometimes - Men don't always want to be the one driving the sex boat. They prefer a woman that "does it all" from time to time. Let him know it's perfectly okay to lay back and enjoy the ride.

TAILS

Contrary to what many believe, women often desire sex just as much as men. They have some pretty vivid and imaginative fantasies that's for sure. The barrier here may be trust. A woman needs to have that trust factor before she will allow herself

46

to "live out" her sexual fantasies. Men on the other hand often don't need that so they are able to head straight to "go" faster. That said, here are a few sexual preferences woman have that you may or may not be aware of.

* Women prefer a well trained tongue - This isn't just about her partner going down on her. But also about complimenting her. Not generic ones but rather genuine personal ones. Women love a man that can focus on something and tell her how much they love it. Maybe it's the dimples at the base of her spine or the curve of her hips. Not downplaying the importance of a good tongue for physical pleasure, but the compliments are going to make it that much better.

* Warm up first and make sure you finish - Women prefer a man that likes to engage in "full-body" lovemaking. This means taking the time to take advantage of all the pleasures of sex. Not just "wham, bam, thank-you mam" all the time. Doesn't mean that isn't hot and sexy from time to time. But there needs to be diversity.

Understand that sex begins for a woman as a state of mind. She enjoys the visual, kisses, slow and soft caressing, touching, sucking and so forth. All of this before the real action begins. A woman likes a man that pays close attention to her, her body and warming her up. Take the time to explore and learn. Communicating his wants and encourage her to open up to you. If you give a little here you're going to get a whole lot more in return. Trust me on this one.

* Take control - A woman can be turned on just by the thought of a man taking control. Show her what you want her to do and guide her. Women want to please just as much or more than men do and more so when they know exactly what you want. Women are intrinsically programmed to nurture and take care of. If you show you have direction and focus she will follow your lead and seek pleasure in this.

Don't ask but "tell" her what you are going to do. If she wants otherwise she will say. Questions are just going to take her focus off of you and the sexual energy you've created.

* Size isn't as important as penis performance - There is so much diversity here and most women don't really have a preference for penis size. They will NEVER tell a man he is "too small," because this would hurt his feelings. Not unless they are a real bitch and don't care.

Yes, a little bigger may make things a little better but more important is how hard the penis is and how well it performs, which is great news because a man really can't control the size of his sex but he can control the his hardness and performance. Woman prefer to avoid sexual discomforts that come with things like pre-mature ejaculation. This isn't fun for anyone and obviously takes points off performance. So it's important if a man does have some sexual dysfunction that he sees a doctor and gets it looked after until he can perform just like the energizer bunny does. That's what a woman prefers.

* Women prefer balance in sex - This means that sex doesn't always have to end in orgasm. Sometimes you may perform oral sex on each other and another time you might just caress and explore each other and that's it. The moment may arise where she wants anal penetration and another a quickie the old-fashioned way.

In other words women prefer a man that doesn't get too caught up in one position or type of sex. There are some men that want a blow-job every time they have sex. Well that gets old fast. Communicate with each other and make sure you don't pressure a woman to do a particular act she doesn't fancy continuously. This is only going to make her feel bad and negative thoughts of falling short are going to pop into her brain.

These will manifest and create a negative energy towards sex that you don't want to be any part of.

Balance is key in everything including sex. Talk to your partner about this and if you're on the same page you've got nothing to worry about.

* Cuddling after sex - Women prefer a guy that doesn't hit the road after sex. Holding, cuddling and caressing is something humans need. After having sex is the perfect time to get connected in a non-sexual basis. This doesn't mean if you've had a long day that you have to snuggle with her for hours. What it means is that taking a few minutes to hold her after sex and tell her how beautiful she is will make you both feel great.

* If you aren't in the mood TELL HER - Believe it or not there are times when a guy just isn't feeling up to sex. Women like it when a guy lets her know this. What this does is establish a deeper trust and it makes her feel better about letting the guy know that her head just isn't in the mood either when this happens. This doesn't mean you can't still be physical with each other because you can by holding hands, kissing, caressing or even just holding hands. It just means that it's okay if you don't feel like actually penetrating her.

*Afterthoughts - Preference is important for both the man and women when looking at how to have great sex. It's about pleasuring both of you. With open communication, give and take and a relaxed and explorative and accepting mindset, you will have great sex and then some.

Benefits

There are so many benefits to having sex on a regular basis. It's not just about the physical release of stress or negative feelings. Or even the immediately boost of confidence you feel when you made your partner orgasm. Your emotional, mental, physical and health is positively reflected with the act of sex.

Here are some of the advantages of sex.

* Lower Blood Pressure - High blood pressure is linked to all sorts of serious disease, illness and conditions. Including cardiovascular disease, diabetes, stroke, Alzheimer's and so many others. Scientific studies have found the bottom number of your blood pressure reading or diastolic blood usually reads

lower when couples live together and engage in sexual activity regularly.

* Less Stress - Stress is a fact of life and by having sex regularly you will lower your stress levels. This is going to help you lower your risk of developing health issues, keep your overall outlook on life more positive, and help you deal with stressful situations more effectively.

* Improves Bladder Control - Tightening and flexing the pelvic muscles during sex is going to help women avoid incontinence when older. It's the same idea as a Kegel exercise, and doing this during sex with the penis deep inside the woman will drive him crazy.

* Get Skinnier - Now this has got to be good incentive to get yourself into the sack. Having sex regularly can burn up to 100 calories in 30 minutes. This may not sound like such a big deal but it all adds up. If you decide to experiment a little more and run with your imagination you can burn a heck of a lot more calories than 100.

* Strengthens Immunity - Immunoglobulin A helps protect you from getting colds and other minor illnesses. Experts agree that having sex at least twice a week will increase this antibody and that means better health for you.

* Improved Confidence and self-esteem - Having better self-esteem is going to better all facets of your life; work, relationships, life direction, productivity, overall happiness and so much more. Studies show that people having sex regularly at least twice a week are happier and more confident about themselves overall. This is beneficial in all areas of life.

* Cardiovascular Benefits - British studies have found people that enjoy sex at a minimum of twice a week long term are half as likely to suffer from a heart attack than those that don't.

Take note also that sex doesn't negatively affect the heart no matter the age.

* Ejaculating More - Less Prostate Cancer - Scientists have discovered there may be a correlation between the number of times a man ejaculates and the development of prostate cancer. In young men, the more they ejaculate the less risk they have of developing prostate cancer later in life. "More" equates to approximately 7 times per month.

* Oxytocin Increase - Oxytocin in often known as the "love" hormone. It helps to build trust. Studies show that after sex women have higher levels of oxytocin and more physical contact and generosity. Something to think about.

* Less Pain More Gain - Endorphins mask pain and sex increases the release of these endorphins, which means if you have sex you are going to register less pain, than if you didn't. This means headaches or PMS symptoms will be minimized for example.

* Improved Sleep - When you orgasm oxytocin in released and this hormone also helps trigger sleep. Improving the quantity and quality of your sleep. Of course better sleep is critical to your overall good health. Helping you control weight by keeping your biorhythm in check, lowering cholesterol and blood pressure and helping to keep your psychosomatic healthy. That's just to start!

* Feel Great - Sex is an exercise and how does exercise make you feel? Great, right? Sex magically leaves you in a "feel good" state where the sky can only be sunny. Now orgasms don't have to happen when having sex. But they are linked directly to an improvement in mental health. Have you ever noticed after great sex you seem to have a perma-smile and natural skip in your step? A simple and effective positive mental plus of coitus.

* Happiness Heighten With Sex - The evidence is in. The happiest people per say are the ones having sex most often. It's a two way street here the right way. Have sex, be happy. Want sex, be happy.

* More Sex, Less Depression - It's proven there's less depression in sexually active people, including those that masturbate regularly. Sex is a release of negative energy that makes room for the positive.

*Afterthoughts - It's tough to find any negatives in sex if you try. Unless you want to argue with the experts, sex is only going to do your mind, body and overall health a favor. Regular sex will reach out and positively touch every aspect of your life and that makes it great.

Know Your Purpose

Knowing your purpose of having sex is going to help you gain satisfaction, unless there is an intention to hurt. This is no right or wrong purpose of sex. Like it or not we're programmed for sex. Sex means survival in the evolutionary sense. Here are a few reasons why people have sex.

* Reaching Goals - Maybe you are trying to make a baby, get revenge on someone, or move up in the popularity rankings.

* Sincere Reasons - These include love, showing commitment and appreciation.

* It's All Physical - You might be having sex to help relieve stress, relax your tired muscles, relieve pain, satisfy your natural curiosity or intrinsic attraction to someone.

* Boost Confidence - There's nothing better than great sex to boost your self-esteem a few notches. People also have sex just because they want their partner to be satisfied and not stray.

HEADS

Men in general are more likely to have opportunistic sex than women. Although studies show that the top three reasons men have sex are for love, physical pleasure and commitment. Surprised?

TAILS

It's fair to say women are more likely to engage in sex for sympathy. But most people won't be surprised woman execute coitus for emotional reasons - love, a proof of loyalty - commitment, and for the physical need - pleasure.

*Afterthoughts - Your reasons are your reasons for having sex and there's nothing wrong with them, so long as your partner doesn't end up getting hurt because of them. Communicate to your partner your purpose, lay all the cards out on the table. This is going to give both of you the "know how" to have great sex.

8- Factors in How to Have Great Sex

There is a multitude of factors that are going to heighten great sex. Some to consider are:

* Need Interest - Which is dependent on money, time and chemistry, and life circumstance.

* **NEW POSITIONS - will expand upon**
* New Places - The bathroom, movie theater, boat, car, ferris wheel, woods, etc.
* Sex Enhancers - Toys - vibrators, dildos, cock rings, artificial vaginas, nipple clamps etc.
- Videos - x-rated, sexual, suggestive, romantic
* Create the Mood - Use candles, quiet music, dim lights, sexy bath, oils etc.
* Role Playing - Living out fantasies - naughty nurse, delivery boy, handcuffs etc.
* How to Deliver - Fast and furiously, slow and sensuous, dictator, controller etc.

This gives you a pretty good idea of a few key factors involved in having great sex. Now we are going to expand upon positions.

Positions

The position in which you have sex has a lot to do with your overall satisfaction. Each person has their personal preference. Maybe one woman likes vaginal penetration with the man on top because this enables the penis to naturally stimulate her clitoris fully, inducing an orgasm more often than not. On the flip side, a man may prefer sex from behind because the erotic thought of taking control and penetrating a defenseless woman from behind may deem pleasurable.

There is no right or wrong position here. You need to experiment and figure out what works for you and your partner. Take turns with picking the position and everybody wins.

HEADS

Some men may say there isn't a position they don't love when it comes to sex. Fair enough. Here are a few positions that more often than not are going to drive a guy crazy. In random order of course.

* Handing Over Control - The woman on top is every man's dream come true. Here the woman gets to do most of the "work." But also the man gets to see every inch of her beautiful body. Giving him the chance to suck on her nipples, play with her clitoris, and of course visualizes that "Cow Girl" dream and make it come true.

* Doggy Style - This position is most definitely a favorite for those boys that enjoy porn. This triggers intrinsic animal lust and passion, entering her from behind while she's on all fours, at his mercy. The man also has the chance to play with her nipples and maybe get her to suck his finger.

* Old-Fashioned Never Grows Old - Men often jump at the chance to be on top. This is the ultimate position of power and control. Something all men yearn for. Calling the shots is just a natural turn-on for a guy.

* Spoon Sex - This intimate position brings a newness to sex as it is. His hands are completely free to roam and all angles are new.

* Lap Wrap - Here the woman gets to literally sit on the guy, facing him and wraps her legs around him. Pushing her hips into him as deep as she likes. Guys like this one because there is a face to face intimacy and he's at her mercy.

* 69 - Guys like this one because they get double the pleasure. The man goes down on the woman while she performs oral sex on him. There are all sorts of variations here, perhaps that's why this one makes the list for the guys.

* Pretzel Sex - This one isn't for everyone. But for those guys that have a flexible partner - you're lucky! There are lots of different options. One is the girl laying on her back with her legs up by her head and beyond, while the guy is penetrating her deeply and pushing forward. This style is also performed while the woman is on her side with her leg up behind her head. Oh what the imagination can manifest.

* Stand-Up Sex - Guys love the feeling of manliness they experience here. Where he can penetrate her on the dryer, maybe pin her to the wall. And if the physical is aligned he might even be able to enter the woman free standing. Talk about a rise.

TAILS

Women may not be known to be as "explorative" as men. But there are a few positions that are preferable for gals.

* Missionary Style - You may think this boring. But many women love this sex position because they get deep penetration, close face to face contact and the erect penis naturally rubs the clit nicely. Not much more needs to be said here.

* Face Down Flat - This position is a girl's favorite because it allows here to feel the full length of a man's body and his hard penis, pinned to the bed face down the man has control of the thrusting. She can wrap her legs backwards around his buttocks and pull him in deeper if she likes. She can also squeeze her buttocks to tighten around his penis. Now that takes skill and is the ultimate pleasure.

* Edge Sex - Here the man can sit on the edge of the bed or chair and she sits facing him on his lap with his penis inside her. This is a great position to have direct clitoral stimulation and also enables her to take him deep into her.

* G-Spot - She lies on her back while he is on his knees facing her. With her buttocks lifted up to his groin and his penis in her. He can grab her feet if he likes while penetrating deep into her G-spot. This also gives him the chance to stimulate her clitoris while thrusting himself deep into her.

* Bent From Behind - Here the woman gets on her hands and knees at the edge of the bed with the guy entering her from behind. She can arch her back and push herself backwards into the thrust. Or he can just push himself forward into her, or both. This one again allows for deep penetration and if you get the perfect angle it really won't take much.

*Afterthoughts - This isn't a book about sexual positions and what you need to keep in mind is if you can imagine it, you can "do" it. Never underestimate the power of the imagination.

Communication

This is without a doubt the most important factor in learning how to have great sex. Without clear communication how to you expect to learn how to have great sex? First off, you want to communicate to each other any concerns about safety. A few concerns are:

- Pregnancy
- STD's
- Emotional issues that may interfere with sex

It's important to communicate to your sexual partner any issues of safety so you set yourself up for great sex.

Gone are the days where you just "did it." When it was embarrassing or forbidden to speak of sex at all because it was thought of as dirty or disgusting but necessary. Thank goodness those days are gone.

Now, how to have great sex is all about communication. You need to let your partner know how you're feeling, what you like, what you want and how to "do" it. Guidance is partial to having great sex.

If you want him to speed up his thrusts and suck your nipples while you're having sex, then that's what you need to communicate to him. If you want her to take you in her mouth and suck gently, then she needs to know.

So "how" can you communicate?

* Verbally
* Physically
* Mindfully

Mindfully

The easiest route to communicate to your partner what you want them to do or how is by telling them, and it doesn't have to be full sentences. That can ruin the mood. More, yes, harder, softer, faster, slower, are all words that will direct your partner to please you. A way of communicating directly what you want so they can deliver.

Physically

By physically moving their hand to that sweet spot on your clitoris you can "show" them what drives you crazy, by moving her physically to a slightly different angle you are teaching her what you want. How are either of you supposed to know what each other desires if you don't at least try and communicate it?

Do you like slow stroking or heavy petting? Showing your partner with your hand or his is going to let him know your preference so he can pleasure you.

Mindfully

Mindfully may seem a little confusing at first. But the power of the mind is incredible. Some people can "think" of what they want their partner to do, combined with specific moans and groans and rhythmic body movements, which will naturally guide their partner to hit the right spots. If you're really good you'll get to the point where you can literally "think" it and it will happen. Don't expect that off the top though, because it rarely happens. Not saying it can't but usually doesn't.

Exploration is also a part of communication. Think of it as brainstorming if you like. This is "free-time" where both you and your partner go over every inch of each other's body exploring. Often this leads to action before you're finished and that's a great thing. You can always go back to the brainstorming after. Getting comfortable with each other visually and physically is going to make your communication much better and your sex too.

*Afterthoughts - Never underestimate the importance of clear and continuous communication. The only way anyone can deliver is to understand and know how to give pleasure in sex. Just because your last boyfriend preferred oral sex over vaginal doesn't mean this is your new boyfriends cup of tea. Maybe your wife used to enjoy when you sucked her nipples. But after having a baby, things changed and now she would rather you just kiss them. That's perfectly okay. Communicating your wants, needs, and desires clearly is going to help manifest great sex.

Final Thoughts

As with life, sex is ever-changing. We all go through life events and changes that will alter our sex lives. This isn't right or wrong, good or bad, it just is. Learning how to have great sex is just as it sounds. You are "learning" different methods of pleasing yourself and your partner in bed.

This involves communicating with each other openly and honestly. If you aren't willing to do this, you aren't going to have great sex, maybe good if you're lucky. Sex always has a purpose and it's important you recognize what your purpose is so you can take the steps to learn how to better your sexual experience and that of your partners.

Listen to each other, learn about each other, ask questions and don't be afraid to try new things and experiment regularly. This is only going to increase the desire to have sex and hence make it even more fulfilling. Positions, preferences, health, knowledge, open-mindedness, drive, purpose, sex meaning and types of sex are all equally important when it comes to learning "how" to better your sex life and make it great.

Add communication to this and you're definitely headed in the "right" direction. Letting your sexual partner know what you want by telling them is critical in learning how to have great sex. The first step to making any sort of sexual experience bigger and better and oh so satisfying.

Printed in Great Britain
by Amazon

47004337R00040